Y0-DOI-383

THE GREAT

GODS & GODDESSES

OF

Egypt

- 🔵 Introduction

- 🔴 Catalogue

- 🟢 Epilogue

Henu
(egypt)

Introduction

A-The origin of the Egyptian Gods & Goddesses

The origin of Ancient Egypt's religion, the development of the early dwellers' belief system and subsequent rise of local deities go back to the early period of prehistoric times. Our knowledge about these archaic times is limited, but archaeological remains and recorded myths from later periods have given us significant clues relating to the birth of Egypt's gods and goddesses.

The ancient people who lived in the Nile Valley revered the impressive forces of surrounding nature. Through his own contemplation and meditation the early dweller of the Nile Valley created a world that reflected his own hopes and fears. Special connections with the stars, the sun, the river and the wind, representing all natural forces, led tot he creation of an astral cult. Archaeological discoveries in Egypt that shed light on the earliest forms of divinities are in many cases representations of animal deities such as the cow, the falcon, the crocodile and the ibis. All represented different aspects of the cosmos and greatly influenced human lives and activities . Evidence from the late prehistoric period of what appears to be ritually buried animals such as cows and rams indicates religious connection well-advised and post-death guardians. Generally speaking, the gods and goddesses of Ancient Egypt are true reflections of Egypt's geography and environment. The important elements that shaped the belief system are simple and powerful: the life cycle of the river from flood to drought to flood again, the sun's rise in the eastern horizon, its setting in the western horizon and its daily travel across the cloudless blue sky.

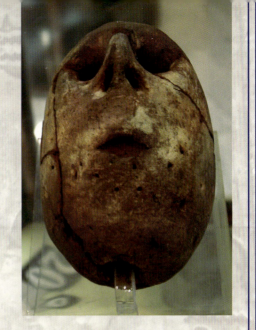

The ancient dwellers of the Nile Valley sought to worship the principal forces of balance and harmony in all aspects of life along the Nile Valley. In Egypt, toward the end of the presynaptic period (ca. 3500 BC), as a result of the development of religious ideas and philosophical contemplations, there evolved two artistic manifestations of the divine human form and animal form. Most scholars date the famous Narmer Palette to the transitional period between the presynaptic and the dynastic eras. One side of the Palette depicts animal divinities powerfully existing beside the image of the King. The falcon is shown grasping enemies by the nose (human in manner); the guardian cow can be seen watching over the Palette (human in manner) and the bull is seen smashing enemies under his feet (human in manner).

B-Ancient Egypt main cult centers / the doctrine
Heliopolis, the powers of the Sun God

An important myth about the creation of the universe developed in the ancient town of Heliopolis. Based on the so called "Ennead" (group of nine) deities headed by the Sun God and his eight descendants, the myth began with Atum who created himself from the primeval waters. Born of the primordial flood at the moment of creation, Atum became the source of all creation from that time on and produced two children Shu, the air, and Tefnut, the moisture.

Indeed it is not clear how Atum created his own children but most scholars point to creation through exhalation of his own bodily fluids or mucus (masturbation, spitting, or sneezing).

This first pair, Shu and Tefnut, also produced their own children, Geb, the earth, and Nut, the sky. They took their places above and below their parents in announcing the beginning of full scale creation: earth, wind, moisture and sky. Later, Geb and Nut produced four of their own children, Osiris, Isis, Seth and Nephthys. These children are metaphorically viewed as the fertile land of Egypt and its surrounding desert. To complete the key elements of life in the Egyptian universe, Horus,the son of Isis and Osiris,was added to the system and was strongly associated with kingship. With the addition of Horus, a strong link was affirmed between the physical creation of Egypt's universe and its social structure and way of life via kingship.

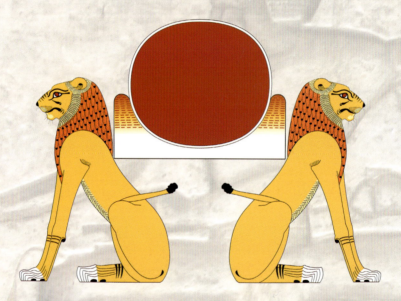

Memphis, the power of intellect

The theological school of the ancient city of Memphis viewed creation from the perspective of the local god Ptah, god of craftsmen, metalworkers and architects. Simply , Ptah was viewed as the maker of all good things in life. We know about creation theory according to Ptah through various records and texts, the most important of which is the Shabaka Stone in the British Museum.

Dating back to the 25th Dynasty, there is an inscription on the stone about creation given by Ptah, revealing that it was he himself who created Atum of Heliopolis " through his heart and through his tongue".

It is important to note that such a "Logos" concept of creation was unique and the first of its kind in the ancient world, far predating the modern doctrine of divine creation. In these words, it is very close philosophically to the creation of the universe according to the Bible when God said "Let there be light, and there was light ". (Genesis 1:3).

Hermopolis the latent powers of the divine

From Middle Egypt, the little town Hermopolis developed another creation myth founded on eight deities, or " Ogdoad ", who represented the principal aspects of the primeval cosmos. The name of the town in Ancient Egypt was Khemnu or "eight town" . According to surviving texts about the Hermopolitan creation myth the eight original deities existed in four pairs of male and female gods, each pair linked to a specific
Aspect of creation
Nun & Naunet - water
Heh & Hauhet - infinity
Kek & Kauket - darkness
Amun & Amaunet - hiddenness
The Ogdoad were regarded as distinct entities and their names were written in masculine and feminine forms to philosophically and metaphorically equate creation as a concept involving sexual union and birth.

C-The nature of the Egyptian Gods

The nature of the gods in Ancient Egypt is truly one of the most fascinating and complex aspects of Ancient Egypt's religion. The concept of God had broad meaning and function because the deities of Ancient Egypt had both human and unique qualities that were always manifested metaphorically in animal shapes and appearances. The Ancient Egyptians however honored and venerated hundreds of deities of all shapes - the invisible divine in various aspects -all possibly manifestations of one God.

In ancient texts, the word used to represent God is Neter, and while the etymology and original meaning is vague, surviving texts from different periods of Ancient Egyptian history clearly show a wide range of usage and meaning of the word. It is more than just God in modern English. In addition to the major gods, the Ancient Egyptians believed in various other types of supernatural beings which are often included in the category and classification of minor deities, such as underworld monsters, demon spirits and ghosts of the deceased. The most feared of these beings were the Bau deities, emanations of the divine always appearing in groups. Powerful magical spells were used to combat these Bau and prevent them from being harmful.

While the Ancient Egyptian pantheon appears to observers to be filled with a wide variety of divinities of all shapes and genders, for the most part Egyptian deities were conceived in logical forms: human (anthropomorphic), animal (zoomorphic) and hybrid or composite. Generally, the cosmic gods and goddesses such as earth, sky , air and moisture were anthropomorphic in form.

The zoomorphic deities , more common in Ancient Egypt, were viewed as male and female according to their apparent characteristic; for example, the male deities often took the form of a bull, ram, or falcon while the female deities were often associated with a cow, vulture, cobra or lioness. Fewer in

number, hybrid or biomorphic deities composed of half human and half animal included various Sphinx statues. It is important to note, that the various shapes and representations of Egyptian gods do not reflect the concept of what the deities actually looked like. Their assigned forms were mere formalities giving visible or at least recognizable appearances to deities that were often were described as hidden, mysterious, and unknown. To be clear, the gods' physical forms were intended only to allow cultic, ceremonial or personal interaction with deities.

D-Manifestations of Gods

In Ancient Egyptian texts, gods were often said to be "rich in names". In the New Kingdom text known as the Litany of Re, the sun god is identified in "all his evolutions" as 75 different deities. The mythical story of Osiris that describes how his body was torn into pieces and scattered throughout all Egypt provides us an example of how one god could easily become many. In the Temple of Edfu we find that the goddess Hathor is represented by as many forms as there are days in the year .Another fascinating example of the multiplicity of divine is found in the god Amun who has many names, some still unknown. The Ancient Egyptians organized their gods and goddesses into groups of triads, tetrads, pentads, hexads, hebdomads, ogdoads and enneads.

The most famous of all groups was eventually the triads group. The number three was utilized by Ancient Egyptians to signify a closed system which was both complete and interactive among its parts. Ancient Egyptian triads have been compared directly to the Christian idea of the Trinity in that the group of three gods were commonly linked as a father - mother - child union. We also find other groupings of archaic, guardian deities like the souls of Pe and Nekhen or the souls of Pe and Heliopolis, all charged with protection of the King and kingship , in addition to the "Followers of Horus". We have another phenomenon in Ancient Egypt called syncretism, the bringing together

of different deities into the manifestation of one god or goddess as a composite form. An important example of this is seen in the merger of two famous gods: Amun and Re, Atum and Khebri, and Re and Horakhty. These mergers sometimes achieve specific theological goals as in the Amun and Re merger where the greatest visible and invisible powers of the world are united. Scholars think that syncretism does not isolate Gods but rather links different deities, the process often creating a third god where there were originally two.

E-Monotheism / the oneness

The connection between monotheism and polytheism in Ancient Egypt has been discussed in detail since the birth of Egyptology.

James Henry Breasted, in his work "The Dawn of Conscience", written in the 1930s, argued that a new religion was introduced in the 18th Dynasty. Pharaoh Akhenaten abandoned Egypt's traditional polytheism and introduced worship centered only on one god, Aten, a belief that was nothing less than a direct precursor of the Judeo - Christian - Islamic monotheism of later history.

In the 1930s the German Egyptologist Hermann Junker suggested that Egyptian religion had in fact originally been monotheistic and it was after the founding of the Egyptian state and rule of the Pharaohs that it eventually degenerated into separate cults.

Siegfried Morenz in the 1960s, drew these arguments together in support of the idea that despite the nearly countless deities of the Ancient Egyptian pantheon, there was a growing awareness of there being only a single God , at least among some Egyptians. Erik Hornung's study in 1971 claimed that the heretic Pharaoh Akhenaten was the only one to clearly approach the concept of one God to the exclusion of many.

F-Transcendence / the forms

Ancient Egyptian texts raise questions about the true nature of deities and also about divine ability of transcendence through time and space. The Leiden Papyrus from 1350 BC says about Amun that "He is hidden from the gods, and his aspect is unknown, he is farther than the sky, he is deeper than the Duat". In such a text we find a clue of Amun's transcendence through the cosmos itself.

G-Worship and Service of the Gods

The Ancient Egyptians believed that the stability of the created world had to be carefully preserved through the support of their deities, for it was the care and sustenance of the gods and the maintenance of cosmic balance that kept chaos and non-being from overwhelming the world. Therefore the Ancient Egyptian concept of religion centered more on individual and collective service to the gods and on right actions than on abstract theological ideas, creeds or tenets of belief. Collective worship of the gods involved constant service through daily cleansing, clothing, feeding and entertainment of their images in formal temple settings as well as in myriad festivals, rituals and mysteries. On the personal level, individuals of all strata of society had access to the gods which, in the later periods of Egyptian history, developed into a close relationship with the divine and eventually led to the concept of personal salvation itself.

H-The Houses of the Gods / the Temples

Ancient Egyptian gods did not mix or interact with their human subjects, rather, contact was usually made in specific contexts and places, the most important of which was the Temple. From the predynastic, small, reed huts to the towering stone structures of the New Kingdom and later period , temples were the focal point of the entire society. Temples were built not just for worship, they functioned as complex symbolic models of the cosmos and acted as interfaces between physical and super natural worlds. Daily, seasonal and special occasion rituals and services in Egyptian temples were enacted regularly to fulfill a deep, religious responsibility for the specific temple god or goddess and served to preserve and sustain his or her existence.

J-Access to the Gods

In the earlier periods of Egyptian history there was often no clear distinction between the priesthood and other members of society, and temple services were conducted by individuals who returned to secular work in their communities after having fulfilled their assigned rotation of duties. However in the New Kingdom and the later period, the priesthood offices and jobs became more professional. The priesthood was considered full-time work and was passed on in a hereditary manner. This created a wide gap between the general population and those involved in formal service of the gods. Only priests were allowed to enter the temple's inner sanctum. Lay people were restricted to leaving their votive offerings or witnessing the festivals and the public procession of the deities in the outer areas of the temple. In many temples lay people were also allowed to go to the special areas where "the hearing ears shrines" were placed in the outer walls.

K-Gifts to the Gods

Devout visitors to temples in Ancient Egypt usually donated two types of offerings or gifts to the gods: perishable offerings such as food, drink or flowers; and nonperishable offerings like simple trinkets, finely carved objects of stone, painted statues and votive stelae (carved, vertical pillars or tablets bearing inscriptions, reliefs or paintings, these are considered the most important votive gifts found in archaeological locations).

L-Kingship and the Gods

The ideology of kingship was nowhere more highly developed in the ancient world than in Egypt, and perhaps at no time in human history was it more deeply intertwined with religious beliefs. To a certain extent many scholars think Egypt's gods cannot be understood without reference to the Egyptian institution of kingship. Living kings served as a bridge between the gods and humanity and could themselves be deified, and deceased kings were regularly deified as they sought to continue their kingship as gods.

In art, images of kings were depicted far larger than their human subjects and on the same scale as the gods themselves, as seen in the inner shrine of the Abu Simbel Temple. The word "netcher" or god in the Ancient Egyptian language was also frequently used as an epithet of kings. Theologically, the dual nature of the living king secured his function in the divine and the human realms , such that neither was ever without the king. There is a clear and constant emphasis throughout most of Egyptian history on the association of the king with the netherworld god Osiris. The role of the king in life fitted the Osiride myth in that while alive, every Pharaoh grew, ruled and represented the early Horus, son of Isis and Osiris, and upon death Pharaoh was united with Osiris in the afterlife.

The Catalogue
Amun

Amun was one of the most important gods of Ancient Egypt. He was mentioned in early dynastic times (late 5th through 6th dynasties) in the well known religious writings called the Pyramid Texts, our main source of knowledge about early Egyptian mythology. Originally Amun was a local god in the area of Luxor, but he rose to being recognized as a state, royal god early in the Middle Kingdom during the 11th Dynasty. He was worshipped mainly in the Temple at Karnak that was said to occupy the " first mound of creation ". Amun was worshipped along with his consort and wife Goddess Mut, and their son Khonsu. He was associated with creation and different manifestations of life, invisibility, fertility and wars. One of his titles is "Amun, rich in names". During the New Kingdom (18th through 20th dynasties) Amun was the lord of all Egyptian gods. Lord of victory and "lover of strength". Amun merged with the god Re making Amun stronger and associating him with afterlife. In the later period Amun was equated with the god Zeus of the Greeks.

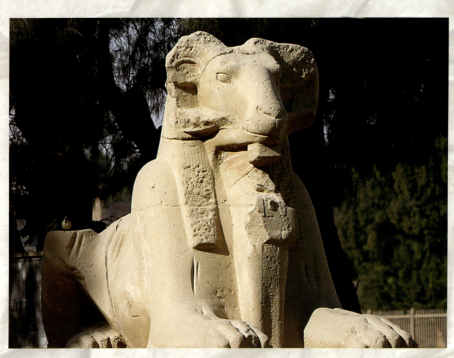

Amun takes various forms and shapes, but commonly in the New Kingdom temples he takes the human shape or "pharaoh's shape" wearing a short skirt and the famous double plumed crown on his head, possibly implying that he was a god of the wind. Normally his body is painted a red color but after the Amarna period (later half of the 18th Dynasty), Amun's skin color began to be shown in a blue color. This shift in color may symbolize his identities as god of air and creation that were associated with water and primeval activity. It may also explain his rare depiction as a goose. Outside the Karnak Temple, we see Amun's most famous animal form, the horned, seated ram emphasizing his vigor as the "secret force of reproduction". Rarely, he takes the shapes of the serpent and the lion.

In ancient Thebes, Amun's main festival, "Opet", took place inside the southern sanctuary of the Temple of Luxor and celebrated his union with his consort, Goddess Mut.

13

Anubis

Anubis, a jackal-headed god and one of the oldest deities from Ancient Egypt, was associated with the burial and afterlife of the King, but this role was extended later to incorporate all the dead. Before the rise of the cult of Osiris in the 6th Dynasty, Anubis had been the most important funerary god. The true meaning and origin of his name is a mystery but several opinions suggest that Anubis' name came from the verb " putrefy ", making his connection to the dead easily understood. As desert animals searched for fresh bodies buried in shallow graves and scavenged for bodies in cemeteries, a defensive magic was needed to protect the dead from attacks of such canines, jackals, and other animals. The Ancient Egyptians feared the source of the threat and entreated Anubis to provide them with protection. From the Old Kingdom's Pyramid Texts, Anubis was often mentioned in connection with the King's burial. In later days, Anubis' cult became strongly associated with Osiris, and many scholars claim that he is Osiris' son. Through this connection Anubis became more correlated with embalming and mummification. He had many titles, one being "foremost of the westerners", announcing Anubis as the leader of the dead in the west where the sun set and the journey of the night began, emphasized particularly in the area of Abydos. "Lord of the sacred land" was a title given to Anubis as master and lord of the desert areas where cemeteries were usually located. Additionally many other funerary titles , "he who is upon his sacred mountain", "ruler of bows", "he who is in the place of embalming" and "foremost of the divine booth" were recorded attributing to Anubis various roles linked to the dead and the cemeteries.

Anubis is usually depicted in the animal form as a black jackal or "sab".

He sometimes appears in other forms of the dog family along with an ever changing tail shape. Some scholars think he was a hybrid animal, part jackal and part dog. He is always black in color, an obvious association representing the color of the fertile earth of Egypt and symbolizing the resurrection of the deceased. A common representation of Anubis is that of a man with the head of the black jackal and with a tail extending behind his skirt. This image is always associated with the mummy's "opening of the mouth" ceremony during funeral rites for the dead when the mummy is delivered to its final resting place in the tomb and the spirit is escorted into the underworld.

Anubis is also linked to the Final Judgment and the Hall of Justice. He is frequently depicted weighing the heart of the deceased against the Feather of Truth, Maat's symbol, on the Scale of Justice and Righteousness. In later days, in Greco-Roman temples, Anubis frequently appears on walls of the "Mamimisi" chapels, where celebrations of the birthplace of the gods occurred. An important association evolved in the myth of Isis and Osiris, when Anubis played the vital role of protecting Isis during her pregnancy leading up to the time when she gave birth to her son Horus. This led to our knowledge of Anubis being the guardian of the King Horus, and later in Alexandria we see images of Anubis in the Catacombs dressed as a warrior with armor, sword and shield. It is the extension of this myth that cast Anubis as a guardian and protector god against evil spirits.

Anubis was worshipped mainly in Cynopolis , "the city of the dog" in Middle Egypt, but in later days his cult was appreciated with shrines and chapels built and dedicated to him throughout Egypt. A wonderful example of Anubis' great importance in the New Kingdom period is the Chapel of Anubis in Hatshepsut's mortuary temple.

The famous jackal-headed masks of Anubis found in Egypt were often worn by priests and embalmers allowing them to impersonate Anubis during embalming ceremonies.

Apis

From the early dynastic period, Apis (Hap to the Ancient Egyptians) was recognized as an important deity in his cult center at Memphis. Apis was merged with God Ptah, the patron god of Memphis, and the priests of Memphis temple chose a special bull with unusual markings as the representation of the god. This sacred bull was worshipped until its death and subsequent embalming and burial at the great Serapeum at Saqqara.

Apis was also associated with the divine power of the King whose physical strength was symbolically associated with Apis. This idea was demonstrated in the great "Sed" festival in Ancient Egypt when, after the death of the divine bull, Apis fused with Osiris in the realm of the netherworld.

The god is usually depicted in its common animal form, the walking bull with the sun disc resting in between his horns and with a white triangle blaze on his forehead. In later days Apis was frequently shown carrying a deceased mummy on his back, running to the tomb.

According to the Palermo Stone (one of seven remaining fragments of a stele from the 5th Dynasty) Apis was mentioned as being worshipped as early as the time of King Den from the 1st Dynasty. According to the Pyramid Texts, the divine bull was also adored in other parts of the Delta, in Sais and Athribis . Historians from the later days who visited Memphis assert that when a divine bull reached the age of 25, it was ritually killed and embalmed in huge celebration. Finally, it was buried in the famous and breathtaking underground cemetery (Serapeum) for sacred bulls in Saqqera. Some exceptional sarcophagi weigh as much as 75 tons

Apophis

The huge serpent Apophis, was the archenemy of God Re, the Sun God, and acted as his opposite in life: he represented darkness, non-being and powers of nothingness. Apophis is thought to have existed since the creation moment, living in the primeval ocean and attacking the peaceful cosmic order mandated by other gods and goddesses. Awareness of Apophis arose during the Middle Kingdom, possibly as a result of the chaos of the Dark Age that followed the Pyramid Age. Our knowledge of Apophis identifies him as an underworld deity. From the funerary texts of the New Kingdom, we learn that he attacked the night barque of Re and tried to prevent Re from reaching the morning sunrise. This great, fearful serpent's terrifying roar echoed through the underworld every night.

Apophis was never worshipped in a temple, and shrines were never built for him. He entered the Ancient Egyptian religion as a god and demon of fear that had to be guarded against. Like Seth, he was associated with darkness, natural hazards and storms.

Therefore special magical spells were composed to guard against his evil acts. These were all collected in the Book of Apophis, dating back to the later period of the New Kingdom. The best preserved spell example is "the overthrowing of Apophis", found in the famous 4th century BC Rhind Papyrus that describes spells of protection against Apophis and other snake manifestations.

20

In the later period the priests in temples read such ritual books and spells daily to protect the temple and the world from the threats of Apophis. Wax models of the serpent were cut into pieces and burnt over fire as a metaphoric ritual of defeating the spirit of Apophis. The nightly threats posed by Apophis on the journey of Re and the other deities who accompanied him, Seth and Thot, are amazing

in detail, and it is interesting to know that only Seth could resist the black magic that hypnotized Re and the other gods on the divine barque. Seth was always depicted in front of the Re Boat, shooting a spear into the mouth of the giant serpent, Apophis, whose deadly efforts to stop or divert the boat were relentless. He coiled his body in the river of the underworld, create a sandbank to stop the boat, he roiled the waters to tip the boat and abort the journey. In the tombs in the Valley of the Kings, the cyclic defeat of Apophis was mythically represented in funerary texts on the walls, most notably, the Book of Gates describes several gods and goddesses celebrating the capture and chopping up of Apophis body into small pieces. Apophis is always depicted as a gigantic snake with

many coils, enormous in size, sometimes shown being cut into pieces or in the process of being killed with knives. Other temple scenes show the King striking a circular, round, ball-like object representing the evil eye of Apophis.

Aten

Aten was known since the Old Kingdom, and his name was mentioned both in the Pyramid Texts and the Coffin Texts of the Middle Kingdom. He was associated with the radiant disc of the sun but not with the sun itself. The rise of Aten as a universal god did not occur until the New Kingdom when Pharaohs of the 18th Dynasty, Thotmosis IV and Amenhotep III, profoundly encouraged the worship of Aten and dedicated significant objects and artifacts to him. The days of Amenhotep IV saw the ultimate elevation of Aten, at which time the god received exceptional royal care and support. Pharaoh Amenhotep IV even changed his name into Akhenaten, but some scholars believe it was in fact Amenhotep III who had originally started the new religion of Aten, and they believe his son and successor simply continued showing respect to his father's desire in worshipping Aten. In history, Akhenaten is always associated with new ideas, artistic style and unique new sculpture style.

The worship of Aten was nothing like any Ancient Egyptian practice: through the great Hymn of Aten we understand the universality of the god who was served directly only by the King and his Queen, Akhenaten and Nefertiti. Despite the fact that there were priests in the Temple of Aten, the King alone was the holder of the god's secrets and knowledge. The high priests of the Aten Temple were called the "the priests of Akhenaten", and the Pharaoh was the sole link between all humans and the invisible divine.

The only other god to be strongly associated with Aten was Re, and one can only look to the royal names of Akhenaten's family members to find Re's attributes strongly present: Nefernefrure and Setepenre. Other cosmic gods and goddesses that were accepted in the new religion were Maat and Shu. The earliest known form of Aten was that of a falcon-headed man, similar to the image of Re and Re-Horakhty, but a major change took place as this form suddenly became the disc of the sun with a cobra at its base. The disc of the sun shines with streaming rays of light ending with little human hands that hold the ankh symbol toward the royal images of the King and the Queen who are standing beneath Aten's image.

From the days of Amenhotep III, cult centers were built for Aten in Heliopolis and other parts of Egypt. During the fifth year of Akhenaten's rule, a large temple was constructed for Aten inside the complex of the Karnak Temple. At this time a new capital, El Amarna (now Mynia), was built in Middle Egypt for the King and his royal family dedicated to his new god and religion "the Horizon of Aten". Two new temples were built, the Great Temple and the Small Temple, both following a new design unlike the layouts of classical temples with their boxy, stone rooms. The new design featured a more open courtyard that allowed the sun's rays to travel throughout all areas of the temple.

Aten's was a private cult exclusively for the royal family and their associates. The nobles of Akhenaten's time copied the great Hymn of Aten from royal texts and included it in their tombs, but there is no real sign of any public practice of the cult of Aten. This situation created

a religious and social vacuum causing people to return to older gods and practices in order to fulfill their religious needs and social habits. Akhenaten's successors moved back to Thebes, the old capital, and to the older religions dedicated to Amun and other deities. Ancient Egyptians reverted to the old practices, renewed in power. Finally, all Aten temples were deserted after Akhenaten's demise, and some were de-constructed and their stones recycled as building materials for new temples to Amun.

Atum

Atum, the deity of Heliopolis, is possibly the oldest of the Egyptian gods. His teachings and doctrine were very powerful in Ancient Egypt during the Old Kingdom (3rd–5th dynasties, ca. 2649–2150 BC).At the center of the Heliopolitan theology, Atum was frequently mentioned in the Pyramid Texts. Atum's most essential nature is that of "the self-engendered one" who created the first gods from his own semen. The word "Tem" the root from which his name originates means "the complete" or "the one who finishes everything". In the Middle Kingdom's Coffin Texts he was acclaimed as the "god of totality". The Heliopolitan cosmogony affirms his nature as the original creator of all elements in the universe.

Atum's dual nature as "the one who completes everything" or "the one who finishes everything" can be understood from the Book of the Dead texts in which Atum states that at the end of the world he will destroy everything he has made and return to his ancient form as the primeval serpent. He is always associated with the primeval mound of creation symbolized by the Benben Rock which was worshiped in the ancient temple at Heliopolis. Throughout Egyptian religious texts we can see that he has powerful ties to the Sun God Re and plays a significant role in the netherworld, as

depicted on walls in the Valley of the Kings. Atum was commonly depicted in the form of a man wearing the double crown of Egypt, linking Upper and Lower Egypt. In tombs, he normally takes the head of a ram, but he also is shown as a serpent, mongoose, lion, bull or even lizard.

Bastet

The original form of Bastet was a lioness-headed goddess, but in later days she came to be portrayed as a cat-headed women or as a cat,more peaceful in nature than her earlier character. In the Pyramid Texts Bastet is credited with a dangerous form and nature.

She appears in many funerary texts associated with Sun God Re as the "Eye of Re", and sometimes with the moon as the "Eye of the Moon". She is possibly a daughter of Re and she eventually kills his dangerous enemy, the serpent, evil Apophis. Toward the later days of Egyptian culture, Bastet was believed to protect women during pregnancy and guard them against evil spirits. She was equated by the Greeks to their Goddess , Artemis.

In her earliest images from the 2nd Dynasty, Bastet is represented as a standing woman with a lioness head. As mentioned before, starting the Middle Kingdom and extending into the New Kingdom, Bastet evolved into a cat-headed woman , often holding the si strum, a metal percussion instrument with a U-shaped frame. Part of her famous iconography as the daughter of Re illustrates her decapitating the Apophis serpent with a knife.

As a very old goddess from Ancient Egypt, her name was recorded on the outer walls of Khafre's valley temple at Giza along with Hathor's. This ancient recording reinforces Bastet's importance dating from the times of the Old Kingdom. Her cult center was in the city of Bubastis (now Tell Basta) in the eastern Delta. While her temple is now severely ruined, it was described several times in the records of early Greek and Roman travelers in the 5th century BC. It was Herodotus who claimed that Bastet's annual feast was the most elaborate religious festival in the northern part of Egypt with thousands of participants and pilgrims.

Special cemeteries for embalmed cats have been found in various parts of Egypt, in Bubastis and Saqqara, honoring the divine cat. Her amulets were common, adored, magical gifts during the new year's time in Ancient Egypt. Bastet's name has been found on ceremonial "new year flasks" as a goddess of protection and fertility and as a guard against the dark forces associated with the "Demon Days" at the end of the Egyptian year.

Bes

The name of this god may have been derived from the verb " besa" which means to protect. Because of Bes' uncertain background and origin, various scholars have classified him with either African or Near Eastern roots. Bes appears on artifacts dating from the Middle Kingdom, and by the New Kingdom and the later period the figures

of Bes had become very popular and widespread, affirming him as one of the most popular deities in Egypt.

Bes was associated with the protection of children, pregnant women and those giving birth. His image is a composite of several gods, including certain features from demonic gods. Bes is usually found in the image of a male lion standing upright on its hind paws. Another image is that of a dwarf with short legs and an oversized head with the face always depicted in a two dimensional view. Notably famous with his thick bearded face and large, protruding, staring eyes and tongue sticking out, he is often shown with a large belly and occasionally with protruding breasts, possibly referring to his role as the guardian of pregnant women. He is commonly shown carrying a musical instrument, likely the harp, or is carrying knives.

Despite the fact that Bes was never worshipped in a formal temple cult, he was widely respected as a protective deity, especially in the later dynastic period. His images and amulets were widely represented in a range of objects within Ancient Egyptian houses, so he was considered a household deity. We have found him on headrests, beds, mirrors and cosmetic items. In later days Bes' popularity spread well beyond Egypt to other Mediterranean countries with his images found in Syria, Cyprus and in Nimrud (now Turkey).

Hapy

Representing the inundation of the Nile, Hapy delivered silt to all Egyptian lands, enriching the soil with fertility. The Ancient Egyptians called the annual flooding of the Nile "the arrival of Hapy", which was such a powerful sign that some of Egypt's texts rate Hapy as the "father of all gods". On the late period Famine Stela in Aswan , he was also called "lord of fishes and birds". Additionally, he has been depicted as an underworld god and a god of sex and fertility.

Hapy was often depicted in the shape of a man with long hair and the breasts of a female. He holds the two famous stems of the Lotus and the Papyrus and binds them together as political symbolism for the unity of Upper and Lower Egypt. Sometimes he is carrying a tray full of offerings, a scene normally carved on the lower part of temple walls, commonly appearing as early as the 5th Dynasty. A very rare image

of Hapy was found in the Temple of Seti I in Abydos, where he was depicted with a double head of a goose.

Hapy was believed to have lived in a cave near Aswan near the Nile's First Cataract, the supposed source of the waters. He exists throughout all Egypt and has been found on walls of nearly all temples but has no specific shrines or services dedicated solely to him.

Hathor

Hathor is not only one of the greatest of goddesses, she is also one of the oldest in Ancient Egypt, appearing in the predynastic era. Her theology grew gradually from the Old Kingdom's Pyramid Texts to the Middle Kingdom's Coffin Texts. During the New Kingdom her importance was such that numerous chapels, shrines and temples were built throughout Egypt dedicated specifically to her. Her most common identity is wife of Horus and her name actually means "the house of Horus". She was worshipped in Dendera, just north of Luxor, with Horus and their son "Ihy". As wife of Horus she is associated with healing, protection and maternity.

Another famous identity of Hathor is that of the sky goddess, an excellent and appropriate home for her husband the falcon. She is both sky goddess and solar goddess and in this regard, she is thought to be the daughter of Re. Her connection with the Sun God was well established in the Old Kingdom and in her role in the daily journey of the sun into the western horizon, she was often represented as a cow, as a guardian mother to kings and a royal nurse. She appears in the Book of the Dead from the New Kingdom as a cow and sometimes as seven cows together, as in the tomb of Nefertari.

Her attribute of beauty is confirmed from the times of the New Kingdom.

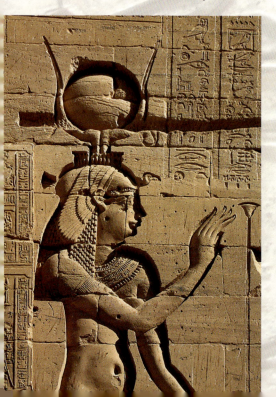

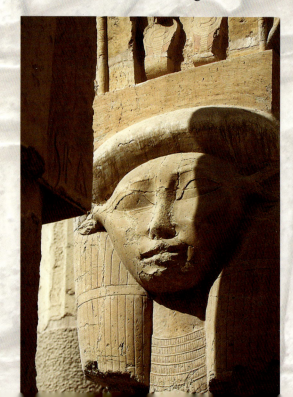

She was often called "the beautiful one" with strong links to love, female sexuality and motherhood . She is often shown next to the kings as a wife or as a guardian mother. It's no wonder the Greeks later identified Hathor with Aphrodite.

Other common features of the great goddess are associated with joy, music and happiness. Other interesting connections include the sycamore tree as Hathor is known as the "Mistress of the Sycamore" .In the Sinai Mountains where turquoise stone is mined, we find a small temple built for Hathor as "Mistress of the Turquoise" .

Her most famous image was a woman with the obvious ears of a cow wearing a long wig bound by a sun disc referring to Re. In the later period, Hathor's image was borrowed many times by the goddess Isis and the two are interchanged in many artistic and carved scenes. In another famous image Hathor is depicted as a cow emerging from a papyrus thicket at the foot of the western mountains of Thebes. Her most rare images are that of lioness, serpent or a sycamore tree.

Hathor's most important religious feast centered on the annual visit she made to the Temple of Horus at Edfu in the third month of the summer season. Before the appearance of the new moon, she spent two weeks at the Temple of Horus to focus on celebrating the renewal of the divine marriage between Hathor and Horus.

Horus

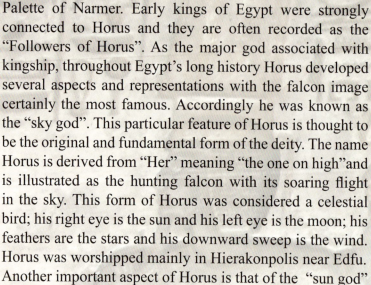

Horus' name and record dates from the beginning of the dynastic era, and we see his falcon image on the 1st Dynasty memorial Palette of Narmer. Early kings of Egypt were strongly connected to Horus and they are often recorded as the "Followers of Horus". As the major god associated with kingship, throughout Egypt's long history Horus developed several aspects and representations with the falcon image certainly the most famous. Accordingly he was known as the "sky god". This particular feature of Horus is thought to be the original and fundamental form of the deity. The name Horus is derived from "Her" meaning "the one on high"and is illustrated as the hunting falcon with its soaring flight in the sky. This form of Horus was considered a celestial bird; his right eye is the sun and his left eye is the moon; his feathers are the stars and his downward sweep is the wind. Horus was worshipped mainly in Hierakonpolis near Edfu.

Another important aspect of Horus is that of the "sun god" .Records from as early as the 1st Dynasty claim that Horus was strongly associated with the Sun God Re and he is shown on the King Den ivory comb as hawk's wings. Horus is also known as Horakhty, "lord of the two horizons and the rising and setting sun" . This celestial aspect was fused with the cult of God Re in Heliopolis and together became a composite of Horus and Re,"Re-Horakhty". Horus was mentioned as a sun god in the Pyramid Texts, and the deceased king was thought to be reborn again in the eastern sky as Horakhty.

Horus most popular representation in the later period was his character as "Son of Isis". According to the famous myth Horus was born to his mother Isis from his father Osiris. Some scholars think that Horus "Son of Isis" was originally a separate deity that was later incorporated and fused with the common form of Horus the "Sun God".

The several aspects of Horus have provided him with various shapes and artistic depictions, most commonly the falcon standing upright. Occasionally Horus was depicted in association with Seth or one of his aspects, sometimes as a falcon-headed crocodile. In later days his image was shown as a man wearing the mask of the falcon wearing the double crown of Upper and Lower Egypt, the white crown and the red crown. This last image became the Horus's popular in most temples and religious centers. Horus religious centers were many and varied according to his multiple identities and forms, complicated by associations and assimilations with other deities. His oldest cult center was in the area of Nekhen, "the city of the Hawk". Hierakonpolis in the Greek language, where the falcon god was worshipped starting in the pre dynastic era.

In the Old Kingdom, he was highly venerated in the north at the site of ancient "Khem", the modern day Ausim, northwest of Giza where he was called Horus Khenty-Khem, "the foremost one of Khem". From the Book of the Dead texts we learn that the ancient delta town of Pe (historically Buto) was given to Horus by the gods of Egypt as a gift and compensation for his eye which was injured or taken away by Seth during the struggle between the two gods. This demonstrates the paramount importance of Horus at various sites in the Delta. In southern Egypt, Horus was associated with the cult of his wife, Hathor, at the Dendera Temple and with his mother, Isis, at the Philae Temple. He was also worshipped in his own Edfu Temple and to a certain extent in Kom Ombo. These temples date from the Ptolemaic period when popular religion in Egypt adopted ceremonial and ritualistic forms. Along with temples in Quban (ancient Baki), Buhen and Aniba, we find temples as far south as Nubia dedicated to Horus. Most important is his inclusion at the great Temple of Ramses II in Abu Simbel.

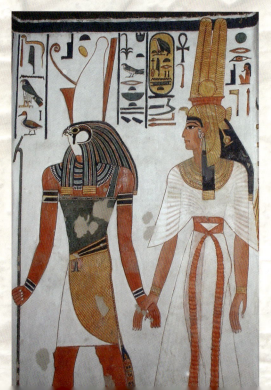

Isis

Isis was the most important deity in later Egyptian days just before the spread of Christianity. There is no precise location in Egypt associated with her story or myth, or with her place of birth and burial. Isis appears suddenly in Egyptian theology around the 5th dynasty in the Pyramid Texts with "her origin shrouded in obscurity". There is no doubt that Isis was highly respected by all Egyptians from the later days of the Old Kingdom right into early Christianity. Her complex role in Egyptian mythology qualified her to merge with other female goddesses like Nut, Bastet, Renenutet, Sot his, and from beyond the borders of Egypt with Astarte, but her fusion in the later Greco-Roman period with the goddess Hathor is her most important syncretism.

Her most important role was being a sister-wife of Osiris according to the Heliopolitan theology of the Sun God Re and his associates. Isis and Osiris were both the children of Nut and Geb, and they ruled Egypt together in the times of mythological kingship. Several accounts of this famous, well narrated story have survived from Ancient Egypt, but Plutarch's version is the most graphic and full account we have today. The vital role Isis played in finding the dismembered parts of her husband Osiris is unmistakably her most important and most famous. Hers was a paramount magic that allowed her to bring Osiris dismembered body together and magically back to life. Her divine conception with Osiris led to pregnancy and the subsequent divine birthing of her child Horus in the marshes of the Delta, where she was hiding from her evil brother Seth. It was in the marshes of the Delta at "Khemnis" that she protected her own son Horus.

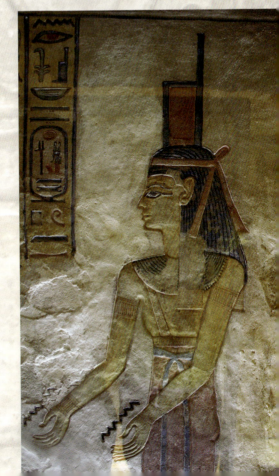

Isis as the guardian mother became a powerful iconography for the goddess and is the reason why Ancient Egyptians were fond of statues and amulets showing the infant Horus nursing on his mother's lap. She protected her son as an infant and healed him from disease (the deadly sting of the scorpion) and this associated her with healing. Isis continued to nurture and guard Horus until he was old enough to avenge his father Osiris.

Her mythic mother-child relationship made Isis the symbolic mother of Kings (every king), and Pharaohs of the Old Kingdom, as described in the Pyramid Texts, along with the New Kingdom Pharaohs who are portrayed as drinking milk from "Isis breasts", thus indicating they are the biological sons of Isis.

Isis has close links to the Sirius Star just as Osiris her husband was equated with the constellation Orion, qualifying both as cosmic gods. Isis merged with Goddess Sothis and was sometimes was called Isis-sothis. We can still see several hymns in her Temple in Philae where we read her saying "I separate the earth from heaven, I show the paths of the stars, I regulate the course of the sun and moon".

Isis and her sister Nephthys were able to embalm Osiris after reassembling all his body parts, there by becoming closely associated with protection of the dead and demonstrated by the iconography of Isis and her sister sitting on both sides of the death bed. They may also take the shape of the kite hovering over corpses of dead people, mourning and grieving.

An interesting note: it may have been the kite, a scavenger bird that eats dead bodies. That was Isis' and Nephthys' guide during their ceaseless search for Osiris body.

Isis is always represented in the shape of a woman with the throne atop her head. In later days she was appointed the horns and the solar disc of Hathor. Less frequently, she was depicted as a scorpion, a kite or a tree goddess (as in the tomb of Tutmosis III in the Valley of the Kings). Her famous magical amulet was called "Tyet" or Isis knot, that was frequently placed on the mummies in the New Kingdom.

Isis' cult was not associated with one particular location in Egypt. From the early dynastic period she was worshipped in private shrines dedicated to her along with other deities. For example, there is a chapel for Isis in the Giza pyramids area from the 21st Dynasty, where she is called "Isis Mistress of the Pyramids". She has a little temple in Behbit El Hagar in the eastern Delta from the days of Nectanebo II, from the 30th Dynasty. Augustus dedicated a chapel to her in Dendera Temple, and a small temple was built for her just south of Luxor at Deir El Shelwit in the Roman period. Her most famous temple was built on the island of Philae south of Aswan that dated back to the days of Nectanebo I from the 30th Dynasty and was completed under the Ptolemies and the Romans. Her cult in Philae continued as late as the 6th century AD, long after all Egypt and the wider Roman world had been converted to Christianity.

The fact that temples and chapels for Isis have been found in Byblos, Iraq, England, Athens, Rome and Ephesus establishes how widespread her influence was in the ancient world from the 2nd century BC through the 6th century AD.

Khnum

Khnum was the god of the First Cataract of the Nile and the inundation that brings life to Egypt every summer. He is the most important ram god in Ancient Egypt, his connection with the ram symbolizing the creative force and power of that animal. His links to the Nile and its fertile soil can be understood through his image as a potter who is said to have shaped all living things upon his wheel. Both identities of Khnum serve the same concept: that of power and of creativity. Khnum was also considered "the soul of Re", and his name was written as "ba" meaning "soul" .This explains the funeral image of the god Re in tombs and in the underworld being depicted as a ram-headed figure. Khnum was worshipped along with two other goddesses, Satis and Anukis, in Aswan on Elephantine Island, near the First Cataract of the Nile.

His most frequent image is a man with a ram head with the horizontal, undulating horns of a sheep. In the later period he was depicted with the short curved horns of the ram, Amen Ram. Khnum held several other titles, one of which was "high of plumes", and he therefore sometimes wears two tall feathers above his head. His most

interesting image showed him with his potter's wheel molding a child, a powerful metaphor for the god's creative merit. This image of Khnum is normally seen inside the Mammisi House, the birthplace of the gods that used as a symbol of the King's birth. The full image of the walking ram is hard to identify solely as Khnum as there are many other deities in Ancient Egypt that take the same ram shape, for example. God Kheryshef.

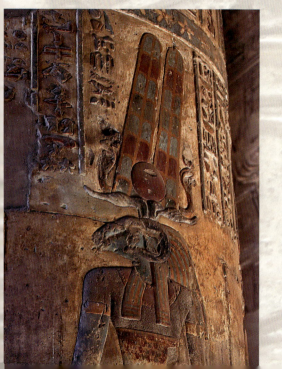

Khnum was mainly worshipped on Elephantine Island in Aswan. A huge cemetery for mummified rams was discovered on the island dating back to the early dynastic period, but other temples dedicated to God Khnum have been discovered in other parts of Egypt. Esna Temple is the best surviving example . giving a clear picture of the cult of Khnum. Known as a " ba", the "potter of mankind" and above all "the controller of the Nile and its annual flood" , his importance was attested to on the famous Famine Stela on Soh el Island in Aswan. As the most important rock graffiti in the area close to the First Cataract of the Nile just south of modern Aswan, the stela's text reveals there was a famine that struck Egypt for seven years. The country was finally saved when Khnum sent the inundation once again. This text is thought to have been copied from an earlier 3rd Dynasty text of King Djoser .

Khonsu

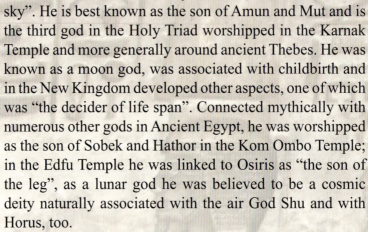

Khonsu's name is derived from the verb "khenes" which means to cross over orto traverse. Khonsu may mean "he who traverses the sky". He is best known as the son of Amun and Mut and is the third god in the Holy Triad worshipped in the Karnak Temple and more generally around ancient Thebes. He was known as a moon god, was associated with childbirth and in the New Kingdom developed other aspects, one of which was "the decider of life span". Connected mythically with numerous other gods in Ancient Egypt, he was worshipped as the son of Sobek and Hathor in the Kom Ombo Temple; in the Edfu Temple he was linked to Osiris as "the son of the leg", as a lunar god he was believed to be a cosmic deity naturally associated with the air God Shu and with Horus, too.

Khonsu is usually depicted as a young man wearing a tightly fitting garment, often with the lunar symbol above his head, the symbolic side lock hair of youth and the curved beard of a deceased god. To demonstrate his association with Osiris and Horus, he holds the crook (symbolizing kingship) and flail (symbolizing fertility) in his hands.

His attributes take various shapes but the most famous is his necklace with its crescent shaped pectoral (also used in Tutankhamen's jewelry). He is also depicted on the walls of tombs and temples with the falcon head, the lunar disc and the crescent.

The Temple of Khonsu was built within the precinct of Karnak Temple which was started in the times of Ramses III and completed in the later period. His great annual festivals in ancient Thebes were always part of the great feasts of the god Amun. Later in the Ptolemaic time, Khonsu was also known as a famous healing god.

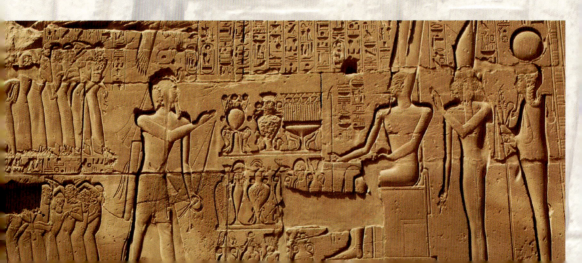

Maat

The goddess Maat is arguably the most important deity to represent the concept of justice and universal cosmic order as described in the Old Kingdom's Pyramid Texts. In the New Kingdom texts we find she is the "daughter of Re". Her husband was the Ibis-headed God Thot. Maat's connection with God Re made her tied to kingship in Ancient Egypt, such that if the Pharaoh is the "Son of Re", he also was considered the "Brother of Maat." She therefore provided legitimacy and efficacy to every Pharaoh's reign, all pharaohs commonly describing themselves as "beloved of Maat".

Maat embraced two important concepts: the first being universal order, harmony and balance, and keeping the principals of justice, truth and righteousness; the second, operating the Court of Judgment in the afterlife as the "Council of Maat" where everyone was to be judged. She was responsible for these vital tasks since the time of original creation. She is always depicted in the form of a woman with a single, tall feather on her head, that feather later becoming her own symbol. Sometimes she appears as a small figure crouching and sitting on the balance scale opposite the heart of the deceased in the Court of Final Judgment. Maat is usually depicted with other gods and goddess in Egyptian temples and has no special temples dedicated solely to her. Her only specific shrine is within the Temple of God Montu in the Karnak area. In the New Kingdom, Maat was frequently offered as a gift by the pharaohs to other gods, especially to Amun in Karnak as a symbol of a Pharaoh's good work and establishing his rule on the principals of Maat. In this regard the goddess is seen by scholars as a gift just like food, wine or jewels.

Nut

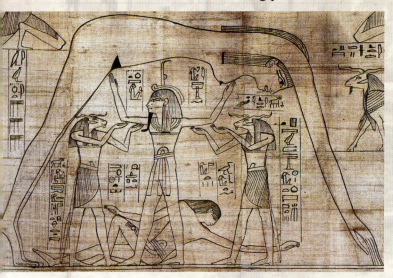

Nut was a member of the great Ennead of Heliopolis, daughter of Shu and Tefnut and represented is the vault of heavens and the separation of the earth from the encircling primeval waters of Chaos, out of which the universe was originally created by Atum. She is the great sky, her laughter is the thunder and her tears are the rain. All heavenly bodies we see in the sky are considered her children, all born from her womb. She has been described as "the cosmic pig who eats her piglets". For the Ancient Egyptian priests, she also represented the Milky Way according to Nut's many images in the Ramessid tombs in the Valley of the Kings that show stars surrounding the goddess as well as on her body.

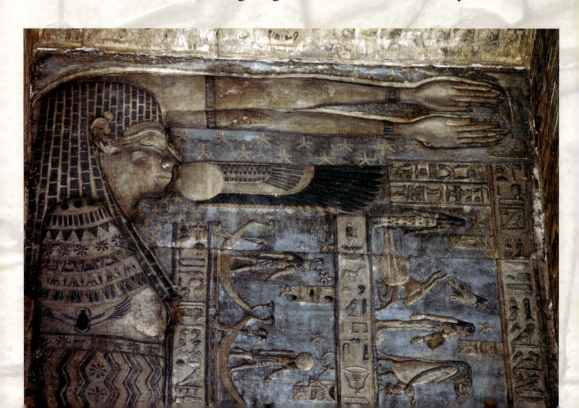

According to the Heliopolitan theology. Goddess Nut united with her brother Geb, the earth god, to produce their children Osiris, Isis, Seth and Nephthys. This myth associated Nut with Osiris as a symbol of resurrection and rebirth. Nut was mentioned over 100 times in the Pyramid Texts and we can clearly understand her impressive role in the resurrection of the King after death "by the power of Mother Nut".

Nut was usually depicted in a female form, bending naked over the earth god Geb. She is shown occasionally being carried by Shu, god of the air, her body elongated such that her hands and feet touch both horizons. When depicted on ceilings of the tombs as two large profile images painted back to back, she represents the day and the night skies. Another common iconography of Nut is a carving on the underside of lids of coffins and sarcophagi, looking straight at the deceased King inside the coffin, possibly suggesting the resurrection of the King through the surrounding body of Nut. She was sometimes shown as a divine cow with her four hooves as the cardinal points of the earth and with several heavenly bodies sailing on boats beneath her body.

Because she was a major cosmic deity, Nut was worshipped in nearly all temples and recorded in all tombs but she had no particular temple of her own.

Osiris

Osiris is arguably the most prominent god of Ancient Egypt. His birth, life and mythical death make him a symbol for royal ideology and the head of Ancient Egypt's popular religion. His subsequent resurrection and afterlife all cloaked him with respect and veneration. The origin of his name in the Egyptian language may come from "useru" meaning "the mighty one". He was associated with the harvest of the fields and the flood of the Nile making him a fertility god with a strong connection to the after life. Osiris was linked to many gods through sharing their attributes and titles. He shared the title "the foremost of the westerners" with God Khenty-Imentiu of Abydos. As a funeral god strongly linked to death, Osiris was the supreme judge of the dead in the afterlife Court of Justice, and he is often titled "Lord of the Living".

We learn from the Pyramid Texts that Osiris was intertwined in myth with his wife Isis and his other siblings, Nephthys and Seth, as well as his son Horus, and this myth encompassed the most extensive cycle in all Ancient Egyptian culture, developed over centuries without any evolving change in its core or its symbolism. It was the Greek writer Plutarch who told the story in its most recent version: Osiris was murdered and dismembered by his brother Seth. Isis and her sister Nephthys searched for the his missing body parts and subsequently found them scattered throughout all of Egypt. After restoring his body parts to a whole. The result was the divine reunion of Isis and Osiris and the conception of Horus, the divine son who avenged his father's murder by defeating his uncle Seth. Afterwards. Horus became the rightful heir to his father Osiris, King of all Egypt .

This story and its powerful meaning and symbolism had great appeal both as a theological rationale for the Egyptian royal lineage and its monarchial system in which the deceased king was equated to and united with Osiris. His throne was taken by his legal heir and legitimate successor, Horus. God Osiris represented the simplest notion of physical salvation available to Ancient Egyptians.

Osiris was linked to many gods in Ancient Egypt, for example, the sacred bull of Memphis, the creation god Ptah, and Sun God Re in the Heliopolitan theological system. In the New Kingdom Osiris was merged together with Re and became lord of heaven and the netherworld. In later days in Alexandria and under the rule of the Ptolemies, Osiris' ultimate fusion took place.

He was introduced with the sacred bull Apis to become the most famous syncretistic hybrid god form in the eastern Mediterranean for several centuries,"Serapis". The Greeks themselves associated Osiris with their own god "Dionysus". Osiris is usually represented in the form of a human mummy with differing skin color, sometimes white (representing the color of mummy wrappings), or black (representing the color of the netherworld and the dark silt of the Nile), and sometimes dark green (representing vegetation and fertility). Whether he is shown standing or sitting, his hands are always projecting from his wrappings grasping the crook and the flail, his two most important objects which became the insignia of pharaonic power. It is rare to see Osiris' image in times of the Old Kingdom (there is only a single image from the time of Pharaoh Djedkare Isesi), but he is frequently depicted in the Middle Kingdom wearing the white crown of Upper Egypt. Possibly indicating the location of his origin. His symbolic form as the pillar "Djed" was very common in the New Kingdom period, and occasionally the pillar itself is provided with human arms holding an "ankh" , the symbol of life.

Osiris' relationship with the sun god Re in the New Kingdom was strong and he was incorporated in several forms of Re, all human in form, such as the human mummy shape with a falcon head, a ram head, or a scarab (as in the tomb of Nefertari) .

The cult of Osiris was established in Ancient Egypt in the Old Kingdom (the 5th Dynasty), existed through the end of the dynastic period of the Pharaohs, and continued to be venerated throughout Egypt in the Greco-Roman period. The cult grew by its own appeal beyond the Egyptian borders along with the cult of Isis, both providing a substantial form of salvation to the ancient world in the first few centuries of the Christian era.

Ptah

Ptah is another one of the oldest Egyptian deities, appearing in the 1st Dynasty and continuing into the later days of Ancient Egyptian culture. Ptah's theology originated in the city of Memphis, evolved for several millennia and merged with other deities. His power and importance seems to increase gradually from the earliest dynastic times to the later, turning him from a minor and local god into one of the major creator gods. Ptah's consort in Memphis was his wife, the lioness goddess Sekhmit. Along with her son Nefertum, they formed the Holy Triad of Memphis. The capital city of Egypt during the age of the pyramids.

"Lord of Memphis " was Ptah's main title in the Old Kingdom, and records show his title as "res inb ef" , meaning "Ptah who is south of his wall", referring to his ancient temple located south of the city wall.

One strange aspect of Ptah is that while he is known to be the god of craftsmen, his true link to craftsmen is uncertain. Perhaps the link goes back to the Old Kingdom's artistic, architectural and culture development and the need for good craftsmen to conduct the large scale civil and funeral projects going on at that time. Ptah's fame as a god of craftsmen may have arisen from his association with workers, artists and jewelers as found in artifacts from the workers' village "Dier El Medina" near the Valley of the Kings in Luxor. The Greeks later connected Ptah with their own smiths' gods " Hephaistos" and "Vulcan" .

Connection with craftsmen may have also helped to develop Ptah's identification as a god of creation, known as "sculptor of the earth" . He has an interesting connection with the god Nun who created everything through uniting with his feminine counterpart Naunet. In many texts, Ptah seems to represent both deities together at the same time as "the ancient one. "or " the primordial creator" .

Ptah was said to have created the world through his thoughts and command's, and as such his creation myth is one of the most intellectual myths to have appeared in Egypt and possibly in the ancient world. Additionally, his myth is connected to modern creation stories in monotheistic religions.

Because of the proximity of Memphis, home of Ptah, to the great cemetery of Saqqara and its God Sokar, Ptah seems to develop a funerary aspect merging with Sokar to become Ptah-Sokar. Sometime later in Egyptian history both gods merged with Osiris to become Ptah-Sokar-Osiris. The mummy form of Ptah clearly demonstrates his funeral nature .

Ptah was known in Ancient Egypt as " the hearer of prayers", "the merciful of face", and "the lord of truth" . Many votive and offering stelae were found near the Temple of Ptah in Memphis and in other places in Egypt, all carved with human ears and dedicated to Ptah as "the ear which hears" . Normally situated inside the main gate of the big temples from the New Kingdom, special shrines for petitions and offerings hosted Ptah statues.

The image of Ptah almost always remains the same from the earliest dynasties through the later days of Egyptian history. A standing mummy figure with both hands protruding from his tightly wrapped clothing, holding his characteristic scepter comprised of the was, ankh and djed (symbolic of power, life and stability), and his head covered with a close fitted skull cap, usually painted blue.

His greatest festival in Memphis was associated with the sacred bull, Apis, that served as a manifestation of Ptah. The embalmed bulls of Ptah were buried in the great cemetery of Saqqara at the marvelous Serapeum chapels of the god Ptah. During the New Kingdom these chapels were found inside nearly every large temple in Egypt including the Karnak Temple complex. We see the god Ptah as one of the four great gods of Egypt inside the sanctuary at Abu Simbel Temple.

Re

Re was arguably one of the most important and well known gods throughout all time in Ancient Egypt. Not only is he a very old deity but he also merged with other deities more often than any other god. As early as the Old Kingdom we find him merged with Horus, the falcon god, to become Re-Horakhty, "the morning sun" , and with Atum as "the evening sun". When Amun became the state supreme god of all Egypt during the Middle and New kingdoms, Re and Amun merged to become the ruling god of all Egypt and its great empire, Amun-Re. As a cosmic god, his power acted on earth and in the underworld at the same time. He developed several characteristics and roles in Ancient Egyptian mythology. He is sometimes called "Re in the Heaven", referring to the mythical story about Re being raised up to the heaven on the back of Goddess Nut in which she becomes Goddess of the Sky and Re becomes God of Heaven.

The name Re simply means "the sun" and sometimes "the eye of the god also called Re". According to the Pyramid Texts, Re travels across the sky, "the celestial ocean" in his day barque or "mandjet" from sunrise to sunset accompanied by his daughter Maat and various other deities. Further, once a king has deceased he must ascend to heaven to embark on the celestial barque of Re to join the divine entourage in heaven.

The manifestation of God Re on earth, the rays of the sun that provide heat and light for every living thing on earth , was highly venerated by Egyptians, and this great life giving force was all attributed to Re.

Re also was strongly associated with the afterlife and the netherworld. As Re fulfilled his daytime journey in the day barque,

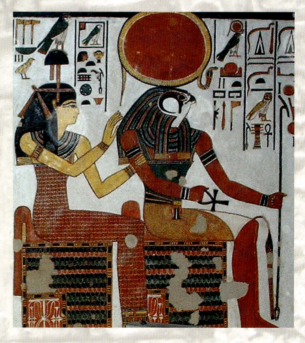

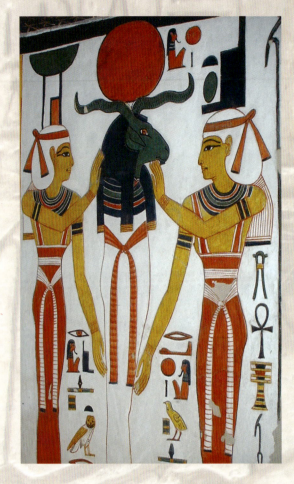

he enters the netherworld to began the night journey from west to east on his other barque, "mesketet" or evening barque, At night Re transformed into a ram-headed god called "the flesh of Re" . The underworld journey has been graphically depicted on walls in the Valley of the Kings, and here we see Re fused with Osiris as " Lord of the Afterlife ". This journey metaphorically represents the resurrection of the god and the triumph of the good gods every night over the serpent Apophis, Re's archenemy in the netherworld.

One of Re's popular characters is the creator god of the universe according to the creation myth of Heliopolis. Re is said to be the creator

who emerged from the primeval waters at the beginning of time. He rested on the first mound on a blossomed lotus and then began the creation of every living thing. Kings of the 5th Dynasty considered Re the father of all kings, and the Pyramid Texts declare the King of Egypt to be the son of Re, in his human form. Manifestations of Re can be as many as the god's own roles and aspects. He takes the shape of the sun with wings or with cobra snakes. He also takes the shape of a man with a falcon head, ram head or scarab, sometimes a combination of all. His merging with Amun at Karnak was the most celebrated image of the god in the New Kingdom.

His role as a netherworld deity in connection with Osiris is powerful in the Valley of the Kings where he takes on multiple forms and symbolic images. There, the path of the Sun God's journey through the underworld is defined and enhanced by the yellow gold colored walls themselves. Royal cartouches used a solar symbol to artistically represent the fusion of the deceased Pharaoh with the Sun God on the underworld journey. Solar symbols are the most prevalent elements used in Egyptian iconography and we find them in a wider range of contexts than any other religious symbol. The earliest record of God Re in Ancient Egypt appeared in the 2nd Dynasty. King Reneb, but by the time of Khafre in the 4th Dynasty Re evidently reached his peak as the King officially took the title "Son of Re". By the 5th Dynasty the god officially became the state god of Egypt, and sun temples and masonry obelisks were specially built for Re as part of the kings' funeral complex beside their own pyramids at Abu Sir. A great temple was built for Re at Heliopolis, and its remains still stand today. Small temples and shrines were built throughout the country dedicated to Re and his other manifestations. Because Re was at one time the State God, his power and presence throughout Egyptian history is confirmed.

Sekhmet

Sekhmet is the most important and famous lioness-headed goddess from Ancient Egypt, and due to her strong relationship with her father Re, she was known as the " Eye of Re " in the Pyramid Texts. Her two contradicting characteristics make her quite fascinating. First, she was associated with destructiveness and fear as "the wrath of God Re", and paradoxically she also possessed the power of protection and healing. Her name means " the powerful ", and because of her myth as destroyer of mankind, Sekhmet was adopted by Egyptian kings as patroness of the military and symbol of their power in battle. Ancient Egyptians believed the hot, excruciating desert wind to be the " breathe of Sekhmet " . In this regard we can understand her association with plagues and disease. Oddly, she was at the same time the patron goddess of healing and was known as "Sekhmet, mistress of life" .

Sekhmet was worshipped in Memphis as the consort of God Ptah and together they had a son, the god Nefertem. Sekhmet merged later with Mut, the famous Theban goddess. She is often depicted as lioness-headed women with a long wig and solar disc of Re on top of her head. Her dress is usually red in color, the color of her own destructive nature or blood color. She has been called the " mistress of the red linen " .

Sometimes her garment has a rosette over each nipple, a mysterious symbol suggesting an astronomical sign of the "shoulder star" of the constellation Leo; this has been recorded in Egyptian astronomical paintings in the times of Amenhotep III. During his reign there were hundreds of Sekhmet statues in the Temple of Mut at Karnak and in the Pharaoh's mortuary temple on the Nile's West Bank at Thebes.

 Sekhmet was worshipped mainly in Memphis along with her husband Ptah and their son, Nefertem, but many chapels for Sekhmet have been found in other parts of Egypt. The earliest record of Sekhmet dates back to the Old Kingdom in Abu Sir , where a chapel was built in her honor during the 5th Dynasty. In later days Sekhmet played an important role in the magical aspect of medicine

and through rites and spells was known as "appeasing Sekhmet" when called upon to heal people during epidemics. In later days' popular religion Sekhmet became an important goddess by means of "the seven arrows of Sekhmet" spell which was believed to bring bad luck or fortunes. Sekhmet amulets were commonly utilized with charms and magical spells to protect against evil forces and the wrath of the gods. People also used to wear a piece of cloth upon which a special spell was in scripted. Another of Sekhmet's spells was called "the book of the last day of the year" worn around the neck for protection during the dangerous times of the year - the end of the year in Ancient Egypt was considered a potentially dangerous time known as the "Demons' Days". Strangely, this practice was associated with Sekhmet and her mystical powers.

Seshat

Literally , Seshat's name means " the female scribe ", and she is the goddess of writing and all forms of notation. " She who is foremost in the house of books ", was responsible for all record keeping, accounting and inventories. Her earliest record in Ancient Egypt dated back to the 2nd Dynasty in the days of King Khasekhemwy. In the famous "stretching of the cord" ceremony, her association with construction and builders was affirmed and attested in royal recordings from the Old Kingdom and the Middle Kingdom. In New Kingdom temples, Seshat frequently appears on walls witnessing and recording the Pharaoh's regnal years and jubilees on the divine persea tree, the tree of life. Seshat was also strongly associated with Thot, the god of knowledge, perhaps his sister or daughter.

The goddess is always depicted as a women wearing a leopard skin over her robe along with a wig and headdress. Atop her head there is an obscure symbol or emblem of a star or rosette, a " seven-pointed star " . Seshat is usually depicted holding a notched palm rib on which she writes about the regnal years of Pharaohs. She is sometimes associated with scenes of temple construction in which she holds the stake and mallet and stretches the "cord" to mark the perimeters of a new temple.

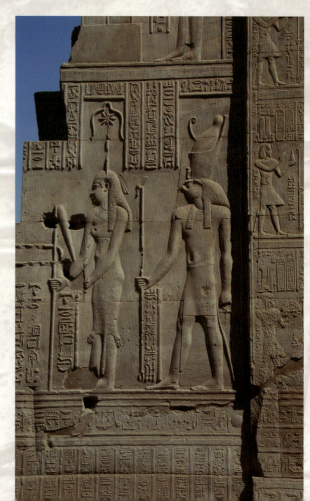

Despite being a goddess of official buildings, we have found no temples specifically consecrated for her, but she did exist in every temple performing foundation ceremonies and celebrating Pharaohs' Jubilees.

Seth

From the earliest days of Ancient Egyptian history, Seth seems to be a god of the desert associated with forces of disorder, chaos and confusion in the world . He first appeared on an ivory mace head in the time of King Scorpion as early as 3500 BC before the rise of the dynastic period. Seth appeared again , together with God Horus on the "serekh", royal seal, two of the 2nd Dynasty rulers Peribsen and Khaesekhemwy.As a prominent god in the Old Kingdom, Seth's name was often mentioned in the Pyramid Texts and his myth was included in the Heliopolitan Ennead as the son of Geb and Nut and younger brother of Osiris.

As Osiris' opponent, Seth was upgraded to be the main deity during the Hyksos period. The Hyksos rulers identified Seth with their god Baal, and he was worshipped mainly in the Delta region where the Hyksos established their capital, Awaris. However with the rise of the New Kingdom, Seth's power was somehow diminished, and it was not until the Ramessid period that Seth rose again to have Pharaoh's name become associated with the god Seth, Seti-Sethnakht.

In later dynastic times, Seth's power declined as a result of Egypt's general political decline and waves of foreign invasion. Seth became associated with the desert and foreign lands. However the fascination with Seth and his dual nature as an ominous and at the same time protecting god remained in Egypt's popular religion. His title reflected his interesting character, "god of violence, chaos and confusion" . He was associated with the color red as an ill-tempered god who personified rage, anger and evil.

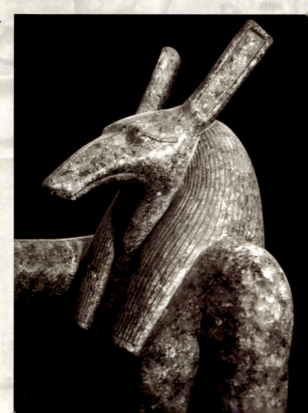

He is virtually the opposite of Goddess Maat who represents order and harmony of the universe. Seth is the lord of the desert, " red land ", versus the green of vegetation in the Nile Valley represented by Osiris. In this context, Seth assumes the balance of life against Maat and Osiris, suggesting the most fundamental concept of the eternal struggle between good and evil, stability and chaos versus disorder in cosmos.

Throughout the course of history, Seth's character gained new associations, and in the New Kingdom Seth was described in funerary texts as a powerful netherworld deity who captured deceased souls. He was also associated with crimes, illness, civil strife including foreign invasions and threats, raging seas, high typhoons and desert storms. The Greeks identified Seth with their angry and rebellious God Typhon. Seth was known as " god of strength , cunning and protective power " which demonstrates that he did also have positive characteristics. His scepter was always the symbol of power and strength which is why Ancient Egyptians linked Seth to hard metals like iron, called "the bones of Seth" referring to its toughness and strength.

Seth is a very old deity usually depicted in an animal form with a long curved head, tall ears, an arrow-like, forked tail and with a canine body. Standing or seated the Seth animal was common until the Middle Kingdom when Seth's image evolved into a human body but retained the head of the creature. Beneath Pharaohs' statues, Seth was shown standing and facing Horus. Together they tie the Lotus and Papyrus plants as symbols of the political unification of the lands of Upper and Lower Egypt, "sema tawy" . The human body with the animal head became the common image of Seth from the New Kingdom onward, but there is one rare and bizarre image of Seth as a winged figure slaying the serpent evil Apophis that can be seen in the Temple of Hibis at the El Kharga Oasis.

Seth was considered an Upper Egyptian god and had several cult centers in various parts of the country to counter Horus as Lord of Lower Egypt. The earliest temple dedicated to Seth in Upper Egypt was at Wadi Hammat, about 30 kilometers north of Luxor, also called the site of Nubt or Ombus in Greek time. It was the place in the desert where Seth was mythically born. Certain animals and birds were sacrificed to Seth in the "slaughter of the red ox" and the "strangling of desert bird", but the most famous ritual associated specifically with Seth was the "hunting of the hippopotamus".

Sobek

Sobek's name means "crocodile", and as an old god in Ancient Egypt, he was associated with the river, the water and the primeval mound, the first mound of creation of the world. According to the Pyramid Texts , Sobek was the son of Goddess Neith and he was called " the raging one" . He is also strongly connected to virility and fertility. Ancient texts mentioned him as "Lord of the Bakhu" , the mythical mountain on the distant horizon where his temple exists, built of carnelian stone. Sobek's most important fusion was with Sun God Re to form Sobek-Re. Later in the Greek period, Sobek was associated with the Greek's God Helios .

Sobek is always depicted as a crocodile seated on a shrine or altar, and on walls of temples he is commonly recorded as a crocodile-headed man, green in color, the "green of plume".

The god's rise in Egypt dates from the Middle Kingdom and numerous names of kings were attributed to the god,such as "Sobekneferu" and "Sobekhotep" in the 13th Dynasty. The main cult centers of Sobek were in the area of ancient "Shedet" , the Fayoum Oasis now, and in Kom Ombo in Upper Egypt. The first

site is an area of marshes where large numbers of crocodiles were thought to be breeding in the swampy marches of the oasis, and the second site in Kom Ombo was where an annual lagoon was created by the inundation of the Nile, a perfect habitat for crocodiles and their breeding. These are the only two sites where we find temples dedicated to Sobek. It is important to mention that all of Sobek's temples were provided with small pools containing sacred crocodiles that were raised and served until their death and finally were ritually embalmed and buried in the designated temple cemetery.

Sokar

S okar was an ancient falcon god worshipped mainly in the area of Memphis. He was gradually associated with and gave his name to its cemetery, Saqqara. Sokar also was associated with the afterlife and in the Pyramid Texts we learn that after death the deceased king was to be raised in the "Benu Barque" of Sokar. Sokar was known as "he of Rosetau", the entrance of the Saqqara necropolis and the netherworld somewhere at the Giza Plateau. His connection with Memphis made Sokar strongly linked to the cult of Ptah and also to Osiris as Lord of the Afterlife. There was an incredible merger among the three gods, Sokar, Ptah and Osiris, and this burgeoned into powerful funerary iconography.

Sokar is normally depicted in the form of the falcon, or as a falcon-headed man, but other representations were very common too. He was often depicted as a funeral mound surmounted with a falcon head, sometimes with the mound set inside a boat and topped with the falcon head - "he who is upon his sand". As the ancient god of the cemetery Sokar is sometimes shown as a mummified body with a falcon head. He appears frequently in funeral scenes in the Valley of the Kings, associated with the fifth hour of the night. There exists exceptionally beautiful iconography of Sokar on the silver coffin of Sheshonq II from the 22nd Dynasty in the royal tombs of Tanis.

The main cult center of God Sokar was in Memphis where he was celebrated every year in the fourth month of the spring season, "akhet". Records of Sokar festivals in the New Kingdom survived in the great funerary complex of Medinet Habu and in the Temple of Ramses III. Festivals of Sokar continued to be an important religious and funerary tradition throughout Ancient Egyptian history with pictures of Sokar being carried in his distinctive "Henu Boat".

Thot

Thot, or Djehuty as the Ancient Egyptians called him, was originally the God of the Moon and later on developed a connection with writing, intellect and scribes. His artistic iconography is symbolically represented in two images: the ibis bird and the baboon. Both were connected to the lunar cult in Ancient Egypt. Thot appeared as an ibis on slate palettes from the presynaptic period, and he was frequently associated with Re and his nightly journey through the celestial heaven in the Old Kingdom. Thot was one of the two companions who crossed the sky every night with Re. The Pyramid Texts asserted that the gods were supposed to travel every night on the "wings of Thot" across the "winding waterways" or "rivers of heaven" .

Thot is thought to be the son of Re, but in the famous epic myth of Osiris and the struggle between Horus and Seth, Thot was mentioned as the son of Horus, "born through the head/mind of Seth when he ate the semen of Horus with some lettuce plants". He was said to have healed Horus' injured eye that was associated with the moon (Horus' eyes are the Sun (right) and the Moon (left)) .

Thot was said to have been the sole inventor of the writing system, and his role in the Ennead in the creation myth of Heliopolis was that of the one who records "the divine words" and "lord of time". His responsibility was the assignation of the years of a king's reign. In Egyptian temples, Thot was associated with "the house of life" which functioned as a library. His connection to knowledge and intellect ranked his priests and followers as the intellectual class of Egypt. As Thot commanded magical and esoteric knowledge over other gods and goddesses he was worshipped as the architect of the universe, his wisdom and knowledge raising him to become one of the main afterlife deities. In the Court of Justice where the weighing of the heart takes place, Thot is always seen standing before the Scale of Justice and Truth recording the gods' verdict.

His lunar identity was confirmed as one of his principal aspects in the later period. He was titled "the silver Aten" and equated to God Hermes by the Greeks. His cult in Egypt was associated with two goddesses, Nehemetway who was thought to be his consort and Seshat who was depicted either as his wife or daughter.

Thot's representations as an ibis-headed man was his most common image, but his other form as a baboon was also linked to his lunar and scribal aspects. In the baboon form he is always shown seated with his legs drawn up against his chest. At the Temple of Thot, erected by Amenhotep III in Hermopolis (now El Ashmunein in middle Egypt), we can appreciate the incredible massive 30 ton statue of Thot as a baboon.

In the ibis bird form, Thot may be depicted standing or sitting on a standard. He was also shown in temples holding a notched palm tree and recording the years granted to the King for his reign or writing down the names of the kings on the leaves of the persea tree, the famous tree of life. We can still see Thot in numerous scenes in the Hypostyle Hall in Karnak Temple. Thot also frequently appears with Horus in scenes of purification rituals for the Pharaohs before they enter temples, pouring the ankh sign from sacred water jars.

The main cult center of Thot was "Khemnu" in the Hermopolis area. The site was probably the chief center of worship during the dynastic times, but Thot was not a stranger in the Delta where chapels for him have been found in El Baqlyia village and in the Dakhla Oasis and even in Sinai. That said, the most impressive surviving place dedicated to Thot is Tuna El Gabal, west of the temple at Al Ashmunein, where we have a labyrinth of sacred, underground burials of mummified ibises and baboons. Every year thousands were ritually embalmed and sold to visitors and believers as votive gifts to God Thot in his private catacombs. Catacombs for ibises and baboons have also been found in the Saqqara cemetery. These wonderful burials and festivals continued into the later days, only proving the importance of Thot and his cult and feasts. Both of Thot's forms enjoy strong popularity among Egyptian.

Epilogue

It is almost impossible for modern day researchers to produce a complete list of all Ancient Egyptian deities, and such a list is hard to arrange in alphabetical order due to the diverse spelling of the deities that varies from the original Ancient Egyptian language to modern languages; for example, Amun, Amon or Amen. Another challenge facing compilation of such a list occurs when attempting to classify the gods by their nature. Some are cosmic in nature while others are related to the underworld and funerary in nature, and still others are more ancestral in function and relations. We also find that most deities are connected to one another with very complicated theological ties. They never exist in isolation based solely on their own forms and characters. There exists dynamic evolution among all gods and goddesses making it difficult as well to prepare a list relying on theological classifications.

The Ancient Egyptian deities can be classified in whichever form or

style that provides a minimum of useful understanding and context to their fluid nature. We can categorize them into "male groups" versus "female groups" , "animal gods" and "bird gods" , and beyond these simple groups we find groupings of "reptiles, insects and fish" . Many of the Ancient Egyptian deities adopted several forms and shapes thereby changing their category accordingly.

At the same time, it is impossible to provide a list of all the deities who existed and were recorded in Ancient Egyptian texts, as we have gods and goddesses who were only mentioned once, and others mentioned by their description and not by their name, for example "the one who exists". Such oblique references to many of the Ancient Egyptian deities is always a challenge when trying to include them all as a complete record. To a certain extent, of the thousands of deities that existed, we only see several hundreds on the walls of the temples and tombs, and many of them there share similar images and multiple depictions.

Beyond the small catalog provided in this quick reference to the great gods and goddesses of Ancient Egypt, there are numerous other groups and categories that were also respected and venerated by Ancient Egyptians. For example, the Ennead of Heliopolis, a group of nine gods, was worshipped together as one, as well as each of the nine also being worshipped in their own, individual cults separately. The same is true of the Ogdoad, the group of eight gods from Al Ashmunien. If we move on to the realm of the underworld and its complicated gods and goddesses we find groups like "the caverns deities" and "the twelve hours of the night deities" . In the tombs of the Valley of the Kings there is a large number of "demon deities" and the famous "gate deities" who were responsible for protecting the twelve gates of the underworld and opening them for the Divine Barque of Re and his companion gods. Re and his companions are the only ones who knew the secret names of these gate keepers. They called them by name, their names often taking on horrific meanings like "swallowers of sinners" or "existing on maggots".

There is yet another very interesting group of 42 deities who appear only at the Final Judgment in the Hall of Maat in the Court of Justice. This group is responsible for witnessing the deceased's weighing of the heart. Spell #125 in the Book of the Dead provides "the negative confession" or the " declaration of innocence ". This group of deities is always depicted sitting on the top of the "Hall of the Double Truth". These deities were all mentioned by name, and some of them are well known gods and goddesses, like "Nosy" from Heliopolis and "Nefertum" from Memphis, but the rest of the deities' names are basically a description of the god and its character or its responsibility for punishing certain crimes. For example, "Swallower of shades" was responsible for the punishment for stealing, "White in teeth" was required to punish transgression, and "Hot foot"was charged with judging all kinds of neglect. The long list of the gods' names and their responsibilities is fascinating. From such a large group of deities it is clear that in Ancient Egypt the deceased was to be asked about almost every aspect of his life before being allowed to enter the afterlife.

We also have what we call "Nome deities" . Private gods and goddesses were ascribed to all the provinces of Ancient Egypt, and these nomes were recorded as early as the Old Kingdom.There were 22 nomes in Upper Egypt but only 20 in Lower Egypt, each with a designated sign or symbol. These were private deities, worshipped and celebrated only within each one's own province.As a local god or goddess their power and influence is bounded within certain geographical restrictions

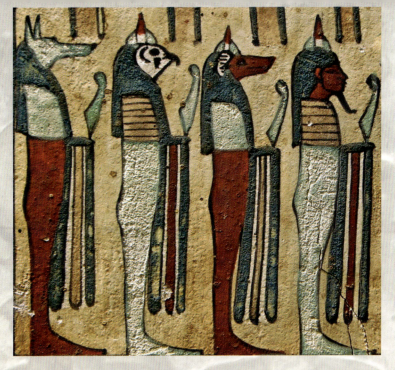

Confusion arises when we discover that many of the local gods are also cosmic gods or gods funeral in nature, like Seth who was the local god of the 11th Province of Upper Egypt, and Anubis who was the local deity of the 17th Province of Upper Egypt. We find gods Thot and Horus respectively, the local deities of the 15th Province and the 17th Province of Lower Egypt.

Another famous group of gods, only four in number , was the "Sons of Horus". Protectors of the mummy's entrails in the Canopic jars, the gods were Imsety, the human-headed god and guarded the liver who himself was thought to be protected by Isis , Hapy, the baboon-headed god who guarded the lungs and was at the same time protected by Nephthys; Duamutef, the jackal-headed god who guarded the stomach and was protected by the goddess Neith; and finally, Qebesenuef, the falcon-headed god who guarded the intestines and was in turn guarded by the goddess Serket.

On the walls of royal tombs, especially during the New Kingdom, we often see the images of three seated human figures, two gods wearing masks, the mask of the Jackal and the mask of the Falcon. The King himself is usually seated between the two archaic deities who were called "the souls of Nekhen and Pe", referring to the divine ancestral souls of Upper and Lower Egypt before their unification in the Pharaoh's dynastic period. Pe, or Buto in Lower Egypt, was depicted as a falcon-headed man, and Nekhen was shown as a jackal-headed figure. They were said to stabilize the reigns of all kings' and power on earth.

The last group of deities I would like to highlight is the most intriguing and challenging of all Egyptian deities: the "Star deities". The Ancient Egyptians recorded many astronomical and astrological images, texts and information on the walls of temples (as in Dendera Temple's Great Hall of Pillars) and tombs (as in the Tomb of Ramses VI in the Valley of the Kings). They mentioned many stars and planets but they were most highly fascinated with "imperishable stars" that never faded or waned, "the northern circumpolar stars" seen in Egypt every night. The Ancient Egyptians called the planet Venus "the morning star", and records from the Middle Kingdom indicate knowledge of at least five other planets called "the stars that know no rest". These planets were given names and depicted on ceilings as part of the night sky deities, traveling on their boats. Mercury was called Sebegu and was associated with God Seth; Venus was called "God of the morning;" Mars was called "Horus the Red", Jupiter was named "Horus who limits the two lands", and Saturn's name was "Horus Bull of Heaven". Other star groups known in Ancient Egypt, like the constellations of Orion, the great Bear, Leo and Draco, were all represented on ceilings of tombs and temples of the New Kingdom. The most important of all the star gods was Sirius whose rising every summer heralded the Nile flood. We find the best examples of the star gods and their different groups in the inner burial chambers of the tombs of Seti I and Ramses VI in the Valley of the Kings.